WITHDRAWN

Team Spirit

THE **M**EMPHIS **G**RIZZLIES

BY

MARK STEWART

Content Consultant
Matt Zeysing
Historian and Archivist
The Naismith Memorial Basketball Hall of Fame

N<small>ORWOOD</small>H<small>OUSE</small>  P<small>RESS</small>

C<small>HICAGO</small>, I<small>LLINOIS</small>

Norwood House Press
P.O. Box 316598
Chicago, Illinois 60631

For information regarding Norwood House Press, please visit our website at:
www.norwoodhousepress.com or call 866-565-2900.

All photos courtesy of Getty Images except the following:
Topps, Inc. (14, 20, 21, 22, 29, 35 left, 37, 43), Author's Collection (16, 18),
Rico/Tag Express (34), Matt Richman (48).
Cover Photo: Joe Murphy/Getty Images
Special thanks to Topps, Inc.

Editor: Mike Kennedy
Designer: Ron Jaffe
Project Management: Black Book Partners, LLC.

Special thanks to Jack Sammons

Library of Congress Cataloging-in-Publication Data

Stewart, Mark, 1960-.
  The Memphis Grizzlies / by Mark Stewart ; content consultant, Matt
Zeysing.
     p. cm. -- (Team spirit)
  Includes bibliographical references and index.
  Summary: "Presents the history and accomplishments of the Memphis
Grizzlies basketball team. Includes highlights of players, coaches, and
awards, quotes, timelines, maps, glossary and websites"--Provided by
publisher.
  ISBN-13: 978-1-59953-284-4 (library edition : alk. paper)
  ISBN-10: 1-59953-284-0 (library edition : alk. paper) 1. Memphis
Grizzlies (Basketball team)--History--Juvenile literature. 2.
Basketball--Tennessee--Memphis--History--Juvenile literature. I. Zeysing,
Matt. II. Title.
  GV885.52.M46 2009
  796.323'640971133--dc22
                                                          2008044292

COVER PHOTO: The Grizzlies celebrate a win during the 2007–08 season.

Table of Contents

SPORTS WORDS & VOCABULARY WORDS: In this book, you will find many words that are new to you. You may also see familiar words used in new ways. The glossary on page 46 gives the meanings of basketball words, as well as "everyday" words that have special basketball meanings. These words appear in **bold type** throughout the book. The glossary on page 47 gives the meanings of vocabulary words that are not related to basketball. They appear in ***bold italic type*** throughout the book.

BASKETBALL SEASONS: Because each basketball season begins late in one year and ends early in the next, seasons are not named after years. Instead, they are written out as two years separated by a dash, for example 1944–45 or 2005–06.

Meet the Grizzlies

No one can remember the last time a grizzly bear wandered out of the Tennessee wilderness. However, no sports fan in Memphis can forget the day the Grizzlies came to town. Ever since the **National Basketball Association (NBA)** put a team in that city, it is all that anyone there can talk about.

Basketball is a big deal in Tennessee, and it just seemed wrong that Memphis had no **professional** team. The NBA corrected that problem at the start of the 21st *century*. That's when the Grizzlies moved south to the United States from Western Canada. Since their move, the Grizzlies have become one of the most talked-about teams in the league.

This book tells the story of the Grizzlies. They are a team on the rise—and on the hunt for NBA glory. Sometimes they may look like cute little cubs standing next to more *experienced* opponents. But make no mistake, there's plenty of fight in these bears.

O.J. Mayo, Mike Conley Jr., and Hakim Warrick go over their game plan during the 2008–09 season.

Way Back When

Most people think of basketball as an "American" sport. The truth is that it has roots in Canada, too. The person who *invented* basketball, Dr. James Naismith, was from Canada. He drew on his experiences as a sports star at McGill University when he wrote down the rules of the sport. *Decades* later, the first NBA game ever played was held in Canada between the Toronto Huskies and the New York Knicks. Back then, the league was called the **Basketball Association of America**.

The Huskies lasted just one year. The NBA did not place another team in Canada until the 1995–96 season. Canadian fans had wanted a team of their own for many years. The league decided to give them two clubs—the Vancouver Grizzlies and the Toronto Raptors. Vancouver fans got very excited when the Grizzlies won their first two games. However, the team soon sank to the bottom of the **standings**.

The Grizzlies built their early **lineups** around a group of experienced guards, including Byron Scott, Greg Anthony, Blue Edwards, Eric Murdock, and Anthony Peeler. Vancouver also **drafted** point guard

Mike Bibby. The team's center was Bryant "Big Country" Reeves. Their top scorer was Shareef Abdur-Rahim, a talented young forward.

After a few disappointing seasons, the Grizzlies seemed to be moving in the right direction. Then disaster struck. The NBA players and owners could not agree on a new contract. The first part of the 1998–99 season was cancelled. Fans in Vancouver were very disappointed.

They became even angrier a year later. The Grizzlies chose high-scoring Steve Francis with the second pick in the 1999 **NBA draft**. Vancouver fans could hardly wait to see Francis and Abdur-Rahim on the court together. Unfortunately, that never happened. Francis said he did not want to join a struggling team, and the Grizzlies traded him away.

Vancouver fans said enough is enough. They lost interest in the Grizzlies. At the end of the 2000–01 season, the team's owner, Michael Heisley, got permission from the NBA to move the **franchise** to Memphis, Tennessee.

LEFT: Mike Bibby, the team's top draft choice in 1998.
ABOVE: Shareef Abdur-Rahim, Vancouver's best scorer in the late 1990s.

The big move brought along big changes. Bibby and Abdur-Rahim were traded. The Grizzlies' new stars were Pau Gasol and Shane Battier. Gasol was an *agile* seven-foot forward from Spain. He was named the NBA's **Rookie of the Year** in 2001–02. Battier had just graduated from Duke University, where he was named **College Player of the Year**.

Next, all-time great Jerry West was hired to run the team. West had been a star for the Los Angeles Lakers. After retiring, he helped build the championship teams that starred Magic Johnson and Kobe Bryant. West hired Hubie Brown to coach the Grizzlies. He also brought in talented players such as Mike Miller, Jason Williams, James Posey, Stromile Swift, and Bobby Jackson. By the 2003–04 season, the Grizzlies became a winning team and made the **playoffs**.

Memphis reached the **postseason** three years in a row. However, the club lost in the first round each time. As Grizzlies fans learned, winning a game when a championship is on the line is very difficult. Still, the Grizzlies had earned the respect of the NBA's players and fans. But they were not able to reach the **NBA Finals**. That would be up to the next *generation* of stars.

LEFT: Pau Gasol floats a shot for two points.   **ABOVE**: Shane Battier, who became a team leader after the Grizzlies moved to Memphis.

The Team Today

To do better in the playoffs, the Grizzlies needed to find new talent to fill out their **roster**. Starting in 2006, the team began drafting and trading for players who could grow up together and be true championship **contenders**. This was not an easy decision. It meant that they would have to give up popular **veterans** such as Pau Gasol. Over the next few years, the Grizzlies began building a new team around exciting young stars Rudy Gay, O.J. Mayo, Mike Conley Jr., and Marc Gasol, Pau's younger brother.

At the beginning of the 2008–09 season, more than half the team was 23 or younger. The Grizzlies' coach, Marc Iavaroni, taught his players to use their energy to gain an advantage against older clubs. In the fourth quarter, when opponents were huffing and puffing, the guys in the Memphis uniforms were just getting started!

Winning with young players can be hard to do because they lack experience. But winning without young talent is difficult, too. Memphis fans have had a lot of fun watching their "kids" grow up and find their way in the NBA.

Rudy Gay and Kyle Lowry celebrate a good play during the 2007–08 season.

Home Court

During their years in Vancouver, the Grizzlies played in General Motors Place. Fans called the arena "The Garage," because General Motors makes cars and trucks. The Grizzlies shared the building with the Canucks hockey team.

The team's first home in Memphis was the Pyramid Arena. It is one of the most interesting buildings in America. Memphis was the name of an ancient Egyptian city, so building a pyramid on the banks of the Mississippi River was a great idea.

In 2004–05, the Grizzlies moved into a new domed arena. It was built near Beale Street, which is the heart of the city's famous music scene. The inside of the team's arena is filled with murals and paintings of Memphis music stars.

BY THE NUMBERS

- *The Grizzlies' arena has 18,119 seats for basketball.*
- *The arena covers 14 acres in downtown Memphis.*
- *The cost of construction for the arena was $250 million.*

The Grizzlies get their fans fired up before a game during the 2006–07 season.

Dressed for Success

When the Grizzlies joined the NBA, they used many of the themes that were common in the Pacific Northwest. The team was named after Canada's largest bear, the grizzly, which stands up to eight feet tall. Vancouver's uniform used Native American symbols. The team name was written in letters made to look like the wood used by the cultures that first settled in the Vancouver area. Team colors included a bright blue-green that made fans think of the Pacific Ocean.

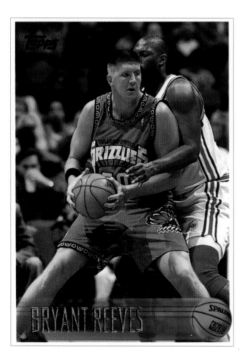

A few years after the Grizzlies moved to Memphis, the team decided to try a new look. In 2004, the Grizzlies unveiled a uniform that used bright white and two shades of blue. The team sometimes wore uniforms that included streaks of yellow and red. The old grizzly bear *logo* was replaced by a more stylish bear's head. The team also used this logo on its shorts.

Bryant Reeves models the blue-green uniform from the team's first season.

UNIFORM BASICS

The basketball uniform is very simple. It consists of a roomy top and baggy shorts.

- The top hangs from the shoulders, with big "scoops" for the arms and neck. This style has not changed much over the years.

- Shorts, however, have changed a lot. They used to be very short, so players could move their legs freely. In the last 20 years, shorts have actually gotten longer and much baggier.

Basketball uniforms look the same as they did long ago ... until you look very closely. In the old days, the shorts had belts and buckles. The tops were made of a thick cotton called "jersey," which got very heavy when players sweated. Later, uniforms were made of shiny *satin*. They may have looked great, but they did not "breathe." Players got very hot! Today, most uniforms are made of *synthetic* materials that soak up sweat and keep the body cool.

Hakim Warrick prepares to shoot a free throw in the Grizzlies' 2007–08 home uniform.

We Won!

The Vancouver Grizzlies took the court for their first NBA game on November 3, 1995. They lined up against the Portland Trailblazers in Portland's new Rose Garden Arena. Trailblazers fans expected a victory. The Grizzlies had won only one **preseason** game and lost seven—including two to Portland.

Vancouver's starting five were guards Greg Anthony and Blue Edwards, forwards Kenny Gattison and Chris King, and center Benoit Benjamin. Each player had plenty of NBA experience, but they were still new to one another. It showed during the first three quarters. The Grizzlies looked unsure at times. They *hesitated* before shooting and made bad passes.

In the fourth quarter, Anthony and **substitute** Byron Scott took over. Both had played in the NBA Finals and were used to being in

ABOVE: A pennant from the team's early days, signed by Bryant Reeves.
RIGHT: Benoit Benjamin rises to block a shot during the 1995–96 season. He was a key contributor to the team in its first year.

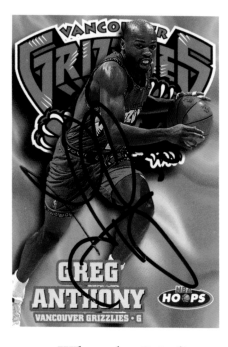

charge. They began feeding the ball to Benjamin near the basket. When the Trailblazers closed in around him, the other Grizzlies on the floor were wide open.

With seven minutes left, the Grizzlies trailed 72–69. From that point on, everything clicked. Vancouver outscored Portland by 15 points and won 92–80. Benjamin finished with 29 points and 13 rebounds. Anthony and Scott combined for 29 points and added 10 **assists**.

When the Grizzlies returned to Vancouver for their home opener on November 5th, the fans gave them a standing *ovation*. Then they settled into their seats to watch the game against the Minnesota Timberwolves. No one really expected another victory, but the Grizzlies stayed close and took the lead in the fourth quarter.

When the final buzzer sounded, the fans were on their feet again. Their team had won its second game in a row, 100–98. This time the Grizzlies did it in **overtime**. The Vancouver guards—Anthony, Scott, Edwards, and Darrick Martin—got the job done. They drove the T-Wolves crazy, scoring 65 points and grabbing 27 rebounds.

ABOVE: A trading card autographed by Greg Anthony.
RIGHT: Blue Edwards shoots a jump shot. He was one of the team's best scorers in 1995–96.

Go-To Guys

To be a true star in the NBA, you need more than a great shot. You have to be a "go-to guy"—someone teammates trust to make the winning play when the seconds are ticking away in a big game. Grizzlies fans have had a lot to cheer about over the years, including these great stars …

THE PIONEERS

BRYANT REEVES   7′ 0″ Center

• BORN: 6/8/1973   • PLAYED FOR TEAM: 1995–96 TO 2000–01

Bryant Reeves was the team's first **draft pick**. His nickname was "Big Country." At seven feet and 275 pounds, he was almost as big as a country! Reeves had a smooth shot, and was not shy about throwing his weight around when a rebound was up for grabs.

BRYANT REEVES
GRIZZLIES' CENTER

SHAREEF ABDUR-RAHIM   6′ 9″ Forward

• BORN: 12/11/1976

• PLAYED FOR TEAM: 1996–97 TO 2000–01

Shareef Abdur-Rahim was the team's first superstar. He set an example for his teammates by working hard in practice. "Reef" was also one of the most well-liked players in the NBA. When he got hot, he could score from anywhere on the court.

MIKE BIBBY   6′ 1″ Guard

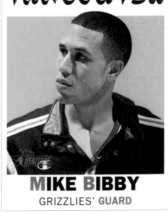

VANCOUVER

MIKE BIBBY
GRIZZLIES' GUARD

- BORN: 5/13/1978
- PLAYED FOR TEAM: 1998–99 TO 2000–01

The Grizzlies were still a struggling team when they drafted Mike Bibby. That was too bad, because he was a **clutch** player who loved to take a game-winning shot. Bibby was the team's top **playmaker** all three years he played in Vancouver.

STROMILE SWIFT   6′ 10″ Forward

- BORN: 11/21/1979
- PLAYED FOR TEAM: 2000–01 TO 2004–05 & 2006–07 TO 2007–08

Stromile Swift was the second player chosen in the 2000 NBA draft. Fans loved his powerful dunks and shot-blocking skills. Swift left the team as a **free agent** in 2005, but the Grizzlies later traded to get him back.

JASON WILLIAMS   6′ 1″ Guard

- BORN: 11/18/1975
- PLAYED FOR TEAM: 2001–02 TO 2004–05

Memphis fans never took their eyes off Jason Williams when he was on the court. At any moment, he was likely to throw an amazing pass or make an incredible shot. Williams led the Grizzlies to their first 50-win season.

LEFT: Bryant Reeves
TOP RIGHT: Mike Bibby   **BOTTOM RIGHT**: Jason Williams

SHANE BATTIER   6′ 8″ Forward

• BORN: 9/9/1978   • PLAYED FOR TEAM: 2001–02 TO 2005–06

Shane Battier was the best player in college basketball during the 2000–01 season. A year later, he was a member of the Grizzlies. Battier was a popular team leader who could fill many roles on the court. He was also an excellent defensive player. In addition, fans loved Battier for his work in the community.

PAU GASOL   7′ 0″ Forward

• BORN: 7/6/1980   • PLAYED FOR TEAM: 2001–02 TO 2007–08

Pau Gasol was an **all-around** star in Spain. Many experts wondered whether he would have the same success in the NBA. It did not take long to find out. Gasol reached 5,000 points and 500 blocks faster than all but nine players in history.

LORENZEN WRIGHT
6′ 11″ Center/Forward

• BORN: 11/4/1975

• PLAYED FOR TEAM: 2001–02 TO 2005–06

Lorenzen Wright was one of the team's most popular players. He had been a star in high school and college in Memphis. Wright could always count on seeing friends and family at home games. Each game, he rewarded the fans with great effort and energy.

ABOVE: Lorenzen Wright   **RIGHT**: Rudy Gay

MIKE MILLER   6´ 8˝ **Forward**

- BORN: 2/19/1980   • PLAYED FOR TEAM: 2002–03 TO 2007–08

Mike Miller mixed confidence and skill to become one of the NBA's best shot-makers. He could power his way to the basket or "stop and pop" from 25 feet. Thanks in large part to Miller, the Grizzlies made the playoffs three years in a row.

RUDY GAY   6´ 8˝ **Forward**

- BORN: 8/17/1986

- FIRST SEASON WITH TEAM: 2006–07

The Grizzlies gave up Shane Battier to get Rudy Gay from the Houston Rockets. Gay showed right away that he was worth the price. After Pau Gasol was traded away, Gay stepped up and became the team's top scorer.

O.J. MAYO   6´ 4˝ **Guard**

- BORN: 11/5/1987

- FIRST SEASON WITH TEAM: 2008–09

The Grizzlies got Ovinton J'Anthony Mayo in an exciting draft-day trade with the Minnesota Timberwolves. "O.J." joined a group of young stars, including Mike Conley Jr., Kyle Lowry, and Darrell Arthur. Memphis fans believed Mayo would become one of the NBA's best guards.

On the Sidelines

The Grizzlies have put a lot of young players in uniform over the years. The team, in turn, has looked for coaches who are good teachers. That list included Brian Winters, Stu Jackson, Brian Hill, and Sidney Lowe.

After moving to Memphis, the Grizzlies decided to go after tough leaders. Hubie Brown and Mike Fratello were great choices to coach the team. Brown had led the Kentucky Colonels to the **American Basketball Association (ABA)** championship in 1975 and was NBA Coach of the Year in 1978. In the 2003–04 season, Brown guided the Grizzlies to the playoffs for the first time.

Brown had to leave the team for health reasons, and Fratello replaced him. He turned the Grizzlies into a good defensive team and led them to the postseason two more times. In 2007, Marc Iavaroni was named head coach of the Grizzlies. He was the right man for a young, athletic team. Iavaroni encouraged the Grizzlies to push the ball up the court and make plays before their opponents could catch their breath.

Marc Iavaroni draws up a play for the Grizzlies during the 2007–08 season.

One Great Day

Mike Miller was a great outside shooter. Yet even he had not gone through a week like the one that started in December of 2006. Twice in a row—against the Toronto Raptors and then the Houston Rockets—Miller made seven **3-pointers** in a game. Each time, he was one long bomb short of tying the Grizzlies' team record of eight. That belonged to Sam Mack, who set the mark in a 1999 game.

Memphis faced the Golden State Warriors in the first game of 2007. Coach Tony Barone told his players to get the ball to Miller whenever he was open. It was good advice. In the first quarter, Miller made a long shot from the right side. In the second quarter, he nailed three more from the same side.

In the second half, the Grizzlies looked for Miller again. He made a 3-pointer from the right corner and another from the right wing. That gave him six for the game. The Warriors had seen enough. Every time Miller set up on the right side, they made sure he was covered.

In the fourth quarter, Miller changed his strategy. He started working to get open on the left side of the court. He made a long

Mike Miller releases a 3-point shot during his record-breaking game in January of 2007.

3-pointer. Then another. And then another. When the final buzzer sounded, Miller had nine 3-pointers. The Grizzlies needed every one of them, too. They won by a score of 144–135, and Miller celebrated his new team record.

Legend Has It

Did the Grizzlies ever trade one brother for another?

LEGEND HAS IT that they did. On February 1, 2008, the Grizzlies sent their best player, Pau Gasol, to the Los Angeles Lakers. Part of that deal gave the Grizzlies the rights to negotiate with Marc Gasol, Pau's younger brother. The Lakers had drafted Marc but were unable to sign him to a contract. Marc agreed to play for the Grizzlies a few months later. Both Gasol brothers were members of Spain's national team, which won the gold medal at the 2006 **World Championship of Basketball**.

ABOVE: Pau and Marc Gasol show off their gold medals from the 2006 World Championship of Basketball.

RIGHT: This trading card shows Pau Gasol when his beard was thick.

Which NBA team gave away free tickets to fans with beards?

LEGEND HAS IT that the Grizzlies did. During the 2005–06 season, Pau Gasol decided to grow a thick beard. Since he was the team's best player, his new look quickly became the talk of Memphis. In January, the Grizzlies announced that anyone who attended a game with a beard would receive a free ticket to another game. Lots of fans—with real beards and fake ones—got free tickets.

Were the Grizzlies almost called the Express?

LEGEND HAS IT that they were. When the Grizzlies moved to Memphis, a lot of fans wanted them to change their name to the Express. Memphis is the home of FedEx (or Federal Express), an overnight delivery company. In the early days of pro basketball, many teams were named after companies. For example, there were teams called the Jeeps, American Gears, and Firestone Non-Skids. The NBA reminded the Grizzlies that this was no longer allowed.

It Really Happened

During their early years, the Grizzlies were very good some nights and very bad other nights. In some games, the Grizzlies were both. On December 1st, 2000, they faced the Indiana Pacers in Vancouver. The Grizzlies trailed the Pacers for most of the game. At the end of the third quarter, Shareef Abdur-Rahim hit a shot to make the score 61–56.

"Reef" was Vancouver's best player. He usually scored around 20 points a game. But his third-quarter basket gave him just eight in this contest. The Pacers had all but shut him down. As the fourth quarter began, coach Sidney Lowe looked his star in the eye and told him to get it going.

What happened next was the most remarkable 12 minutes in team history. Abdur-Rahim could not miss. He made every kind of shot imaginable. The Pacers looked helpless on defense. Meanwhile, no one else on the Grizzlies could make a basket.

With 21 seconds left and the Pacers desperate to stop him, Abdur-Rahim made a long 3-pointer to tie the game 76–76. That sent the game into overtime. Vancouver had scored 20 points in the fourth quarter, and Reef had them all!

Shareef Abdur-Raheem dunks in January of 2001. A month earlier, he set a team scoring record.

"We stopped him in the first half," remembers Indiana coach Isiah Thomas, "but he figured out what we were doing, as great players do."

"I felt with the ball in my hands I could make something happen," Abdur-Rahim recalls.

Abdur-Rahim was now the proud owner of a team record. No other Grizzly had ever scored all of his team's points in a quarter. Unfortunately, the Grizzlies tied an NBA record moments later. They went scoreless in overtime and lost 86–76!

Team Spirit

Memphis is the only NBA team in the part of the country known as the Mid-South Region. Basketball is very popular in this part of the country. The Grizzlies connect with fans in four states—Tennessee, Arkansas, Mississippi, and Missouri.

The team does its best to entertain fans. The Grizz Girls perform dance routines during timeouts. There is also a dance team called the Grannies and Grandpas. They are one of the crowd's favorites. At halftime, the Kings of the Court perform acrobatic dunks. And all game long the team's mascot, Grizz, has fun with the fans. He has been with the team since its days in Vancouver. When the team changed its colors in 2004, Grizz changed colors, too.

The Grizzlies also do a lot to help their fans. The team supports several reading programs in the area, and the players can often be found in schools, reading to students. The players also visit the reading clubs and centers that the team has set up around the city of Memphis.

Grizz leaps through a ring of fire for an amazing dunk.

Timeline

The basketball season is played from October through June. That means each season takes place at the end of one year and the beginning of the next. In this timeline, the accomplishments of the Grizzlies are shown by season.

1995–96
The Grizzlies join the NBA.

1999–00
The Grizzlies make an 11-player trade.

1997–98
Shareef Abdur-Rahim averages 20 points a game.

2001–02
The team moves to Memphis, Tennessee.

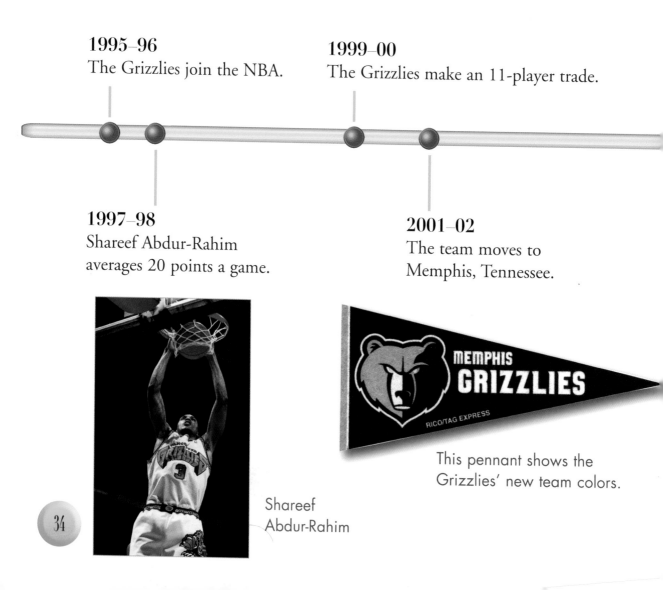

Shareef Abdur-Rahim

MEMPHIS GRIZZLIES

RICO/TAG EXPRESS

This pennant shows the Grizzlies' new team colors.

Stromile Swift, a star for the 2004–05 team.

O.J. Mayo

2004–05
The Grizzlies make the playoffs for the second year in a row.

2008–09
The Grizzlies trade for O.J. Mayo on draft day.

2003–04
Shane Battier is a finalist for the NBA **Sportsmanship Award**.

2006–07
Mike Miller makes nine 3-pointers in a game.

Shane Battier

Fun Facts

LIKE MIKE

Mike Conley Jr. gets his great leaping ability from his dad. Mike Conley Sr. won a gold medal in the triple jump at the 1992 Olympics and a silver medal at the 1984 Olympics. He also won the Celebrity Slam Dunk Contest in 1988, 1989, and 1992.

INTERESTING POINT

When the Grizzlies moved to Memphis, their first home was the Pyramid Arena. At 321 feet tall, it was the sixth-largest pyramid in the world. The tallest is the Great Pyramid of Giza, which is 456 feet tall.

LIVING COLOR

Blue Edwards got his unusual first name when he choked on some food as a baby. His family was amazed at how blue he turned. From that day on, he was no longer known as Theodore. He was simply Blue.

ABOVE: Mike Conley Sr. celebrates his gold medal at the 1992 Olympics.
RIGHT: George Thompson, a star for the Memphis Tams.

WELCOME BACK

The Grizzlies are the second pro basketball team to make Memphis their home. During the early 1970s, the Memphis Pros played there. They were also known as the Tams and Sounds. The team belonged to the ABA.

OVERSEAS SENSATION

In 2008, the Grizzlies signed 7′ 2″ Hamed Haddadi. He was the star of Iran's Olympic basketball team. Haddadi became the first Iranian to play in the NBA.

GUARD M D...

TAMS
GEORGE THOMPSON

TORCHED!

When Pau Gasol dunked, he held the ball as high above his head as he could. Memphis fans called this the Statue of Liberty Dunk.

GOOD AS GOLD

Shareef Abdur-Rahim never enjoyed a winning season with the Grizzlies. But he was not left empty handed during those years. In 2000, he received a gold medal when Team USA won the men's basketball tournament at the *Olympics* in Australia.

Talking Hoops

"We are young. We are athletic. We have talent."

—Rudy Gay, on the team's future

"I really want a team that Memphis will take pride in ... I believe we've started to build a great young team."

—Michael Heisley, on giving fans an exciting team

"Nobody had faith in me when I got here except my team. That's what carried me through all the **transition** problems and adjustments and everything."

—Pau Gasol, on the importance of getting the support of teammates

"I stayed with a dream and it finally came true."

—*O.J. Mayo, on his childhood goal of reaching the NBA*

"We want to attack the opponent. At the same time, we want to make sure we do a great job of setting our defense as quickly as possible."

—*Marc Iavaroni, on taking advantage of the team's speed*

"I feel like if I need to say something, then I am going to say it. I learned that from Hubie Brown."

—*Jason Williams, on being a confident team leader*

LEFT: Rudy Gay soars for a dunk.
ABOVE: O.J. Mayo poses for a picture with teammate Darrell Arthur, another top draft pick in 2008.

For the Record

The great Grizzlies teams and players have left their marks on the record books. These are the "best of the best" …

GRIZZLIES AWARD WINNERS

WINNER	AWARD	SEASON
Pau Gasol	Rookie of the Year	2001–02
Hubie Brown	Coach of the Year	2003–04
Jerry West	Executive of the Year	2003–04
Mike Miller	Sixth Man of the Year*	2005–06

The Sixth Man of the Year award is given to the league's best substitute player.

LEFT: Coach Hubie Brown gives instructions to Jason Williams during 2003–04. Brown was named Coach of the Year that season.
RIGHT: Mike Miller shows off his Sixth Man of the Year trophy with Jerry West.

Pinpoints

The history of a basketball team is made up of many smaller stories. These stories take place all over the map—not just in the city a team calls "home." Match the push-pins on these maps to the Team Facts and you will begin to see the story of the Grizzlies unfold!

TEAM FACTS

1 Memphis, Tennessee—*The Grizzlies have played here since 2001–02.*

2 Marietta, Georgia—*Shareef Abdur-Rahim was born here.*

3 Birmingham, Michigan—*Shane Battier was born here.*

4 Huntington, West Virginia—*O.J. Mayo was born here.*

5 Baltimore, Maryland—*Rudy Gay was born here.*

6 Fort Smith, Arkansas—*Bryant Reeves was born here.*

7 Shreveport, Louisiana—*Stromile Swift was born here.*

8 Mitchell, South Dakota—*Mike Miller was born here.*

9 Ogden, Utah—*Byron Scott was born here.*

10 Las Vegas, Nevada—*Greg Anthony was born here.*

11 Vancouver, British Columbia, Canada—*The Grizzlies played here from 1995–96 to 2000–01.*

12 Barcelona, Spain—*Pau and Marc Gasol were born here.*

Pau Gasol

Play Ball

Basketball is a sport played by two teams of five players. NBA games have four 12-minute quarters—48 minutes in all—and the team that scores the most points when time has run out is the winner. Most baskets count for two points. Players who make shots from beyond the three-point line receive an extra point. Baskets made from the free-throw line count for one point. Free throws are penalty shots awarded to a team, usually after an opponent has committed a foul. A foul is called when one player makes hard contact with another.

Players can move around all they want, but the player with the ball cannot. He must bounce the ball with one hand or the other (but never both) in order to go from one part of the court to another. As long as he keeps "dribbling," he can keep moving.

In the NBA, teams must attempt a shot every 24 seconds, so there is little time to waste. The job of the defense is to make it as difficult as possible to take a good shot—and to grab the ball if the other team shoots and misses.

This may sound simple, but anyone who has played the game knows that basketball can be very complicated. Every player on the court has a job to do. Different players have different strengths and weaknesses. The coach must mix these players in just the right way, and teach them to work together as one.

44

The more you play and watch basketball, the more "little things" you are likely to notice. The next time you are at a game, look for these plays:

PLAY LIST

ALLEY-OOP—A play where the passer throws the ball just to the side of the rim—so a teammate can catch it and dunk in one motion.

BACK-DOOR PLAY—A play where the passer waits for his teammate to fake the defender away from the basket—then throws him the ball when he cuts back toward the basket.

KICK-OUT—A play where the ball-handler waits for the defense to surround him—then quickly passes to a teammate who is open for an outside shot. The ball is not really kicked in this play; the term comes from the action of pinball machines.

NO-LOOK PASS—A play where the passer fools a defender (with his eyes) into covering one teammate—then suddenly passes to another without looking.

PICK-AND-ROLL—A play where one teammate blocks or "picks off" another's defender with his body—then cuts to the basket for a pass in the confusion.

Glossary

BASKETBALL WORDS TO KNOW

3-POINTERS—Baskets made from behind the 3-point line.

ALL-AROUND—Good at all parts of the game.

AMERICAN BASKETBALL ASSOCIATION (ABA)—The basketball league that played for nine seasons starting in 1967. Prior to the 1976–77 season, four ABA teams joined the NBA, and the rest went out of business.

ASSISTS—Passes that lead to successful shots.

BASKETBALL ASSOCIATION OF AMERICA—The league that started in 1946–47 and later became the NBA.

CLUTCH—Able to perform well under pressure.

COLLEGE PLAYER OF THE YEAR—The award given each season to the nation's best college basketball player.

DRAFT PICK—A college player selected or "drafted" by NBA teams each summer.

DRAFTED—Chosen from a group of the best college players. The NBA draft is held each summer.

FRANCHISE—The players, coaches, and business people who make up a team.

FREE AGENT—A player who is allowed to sign with any team that wants him.

LINEUPS—The lists of players who are playing in a game.

NATIONAL BASKETBALL ASSOCIATION (NBA)—The professional league that has been operating since 1946–47.

NBA DRAFT—The annual meeting where teams pick from a group of the best college players.

NBA FINALS—The playoff series that decides the champion of the league.

OVERTIME—The extra period played when a game is tied after 48 minutes.

PLAYMAKER—Someone who helps his teammates score by passing the ball.

PLAYOFFS—The games played after the season to determine the league champion.

POSTSEASON—Another term for playoffs.

PRESEASON—Taking place before the regular season. Wins and losses in the preseason do not count.

PROFESSIONAL—A player or team that plays a sport for money. College players are not paid, so they are considered "amateurs."

ROOKIE OF THE YEAR—The annual award given to the league's best first-year player.

ROSTER—The list of players on a team.

SPORTSMANSHIP AWARD—The award given to the player who shows the best attitude on the court.

STANDINGS—A daily list of teams, starting with the team with the best record and ending with the team with the worst record.

SUBSTITUTE—A player who begins most games on the bench.

VETERANS—Players with great experience.

WORLD CHAMPIONSHIP OF BASKETBALL—The tournament for national teams from countries all around the world.

OTHER WORDS TO KNOW

AGILE—Quick and graceful.

CENTURY—A period of 100 years.

CONTENDERS—People who compete for a championship.

DECADES—Periods of 10 years; also specific periods, such as the 1950s.

EXPERIENCED—Having knowledge and skill in a job.

GENERATION—The period of years roughly equal to the time it takes for a person to be born, grow up, and have children.

HESITATED—Paused.

INVENTED—Created through clever thinking.

LOGO—A symbol or design that represents a company or team.

OLYMPICS—An international sports competition held every four years.

OVATION—A long, loud cheer.

SATIN—A smooth, shiny fabric.

SYNTHETIC—Made in a laboratory, not in nature.

TRANSITION—A change from one place to another.

Places to Go

ON THE ROAD

MEMPHIS GRIZZLIES
191 Beale Street
Memphis, Tennessee 38103
(901) 205-1234

**NAISMITH MEMORIAL
BASKETBALL HALL OF FAME**
1000 West Columbus Avenue
Springfield, Massachusetts 01105
(877) 4HOOPLA

ON THE WEB

THE NATIONAL BASKETBALL ASSOCIATION   www.nba.com
  • *Learn more about the league's teams, players, and history*

THE MEMPHIS GRIZZLIES   www.nba.com/grizzlies
  • *Learn more about the Grizzlies*

THE BASKETBALL HALL OF FAME   www.hoophall.com
  • *Learn more about history's greatest players*

ON THE BOOKSHELF

To learn more about the sport of basketball, look for these books at your library or bookstore:

  • Hareas, John. *Basketball*. New York, New York: DK, 2005.

  • Hughes, Morgan. *Basketball*. Vero Beach, Florida: Rourke Publishing, 2005.

  • Thomas, Keltie. *How Basketball Works*. Berkeley, California: Maple Tree Press, distributed through Publishers Group West, 2005.

Index

The Team

MARK STEWART has written more than 20 books on basketball, and over 100 sports books for kids. He grew up in New York City during the 1960s rooting for the Knicks and Nets, and now takes his two daughters, Mariah and Rachel, to watch them play. Mark comes from a family of writers. His grandfather was Sunday Editor of *The New York Times* and his mother was Articles Editor of *The Ladies Home Journal* and *McCall's*. Mark has profiled hundreds of athletes over the last 20 years. He has also written several books about his native New York, and New Jersey, his home today. Mark is a graduate of Duke University, with a degree in history. He lives with his daughters and wife, Sarah, overlooking Sandy Hook, New Jersey.

MATT ZEYSING is the resident historian at the Basketball Hall of Fame in Springfield, Massachusetts. His research interests include the origins of the game of basketball, the development of professional basketball in the first half of the twentieth century, and the culture and meaning of basketball in American society.